KidLit·

Elvis Presley for Kids

A Biography of Elvis Presley Just for Kids!

Sara Presley

KidLit-O Press

www.KidLito.com

© 2013. All Rights Reserved

Table of Contents

About

KidLit-o was started for one simple reason: our kids. They wanted to find a way to introduce classic literature to their children.

Books in this series take all the classics that they love and make them age appropriate for a younger audience—while still keeping the integrity and style of the original.

We hope you and you children enjoy them. We love feedback, so if you have a question or comment, stop by our website!

Introduction: Childhood

It was January 8, 1935 in a small two-room house, located in Tupelo, Mississippi that Elvis Aaron Presley was born. His life started with tragedy when his twin brother Jessie Garon didn't survive and was stillborn. However, Elvis was in excellent health and would stay that way for many years. Elvis had a destiny on earth, to become the king of Rock & Roll, and would touch the hearts of millions in life and in death.

This is his story.

For the first ten years or so of Elvis's life in Tupelo Mississippi, he was surrounded by nearby relatives, all of working class families. Aunts, uncles, grandparents and many cousins surrounded him, even though his parents moved many times around town. As the center of attention for his parents, Vernon and Gladys, Elvis was also surrounded by music in those early years at the Assembly of God Church. The gospel music, and blues by black musicians influenced his early appreciation of religion and music. If that wasn't enough, his parents played country music around the house, which became part of the roots of his life.

Chapter 1: First Recordings

Elvis earned his first $5.00 in 1946 when he performed in the talent contest at the local Fair & Dairy Show, singing "Old Shep" into a microphone while standing on a chair. Although he didn't receive a cash prize, he did receive the $5.00 in tickets for the rides at the fair. A year later in 1946, because of money being short in the Presley family, Elvis didn't get the bicycle he really wanted. Instead, his Mom talked Elvis into something that would become a symbol of his life, his first guitar. For $12.95, Elvis got his first guitar at the Tupelo Hardware Store, and this event set the path for his life ahead.

In search of a better life, the Presley family pack up their belongings in the 1939 Plymouth, and move to Memphis, Tennessee in November of 1948. Before leaving Elvis performed the song "Leaf on a Tree" with his guitar for his high school class as his goodbye. Many of the family relatives followed them to Memphis over the next years.

From the time the family arrived in Memphis through 1953, the Presley's experienced very hard times, not quite what they expected. They found themselves living in the poorest of neighborhoods, including public housing. Elvis's parents try hard to support the family, moving from one job to the next, and Elvis works a variety of jobs to help support his family and himself. It is during these tough years that Elvis truly starts to develop into the man we came to know. He absorbed the white and black gospel songs he listened to in downtown Memphis. He changes how he dresses, grows his hair longer than acceptable in those days, and grows some serious sideburns. Elvis becomes someone who stands out from the rest of the high school kids his age, as totally different.

When Elvis turn 18 on January 19, 1953, he registered for the Selective Service System, as was the law back then. Like all young men in those days, if you were in good health, you were expected to serve two years active duty and four years reserve duty. This Selective Service draft system continued until after the Vietnam War, when it was discontinued. Elvis was assigned the Selective Service number of 40-86-35-16. Elvis wasn't drafted then and went on to finish and graduate from L.C. Humes High School.

It was while attending L.C. Humes High School in Memphis that Elvis signed up for the school talent show, and this well liked "different kid" rocked the crowd and was chosen as the winner. The crowd demanded an encore, and Elvis delivered.

In 1956, Elvis had his first significant break and received national recognition with the release of his hit song Heartbreak Hotel. The song was actually inspired by newspaper article he had read. This was also the year that his nickname "Elvis the pelvis" started and stuck. This happened because while performing on the Milton Berle Show on TV, Milton had asked Elvis to sing without his guitar. What caused the commotion was the world saw Elvis and his gyrating hips moving to the music. This was something Elvis had done for years, as he said, he just felt the music, and that's how it moved him. Unfortunately, the world had been listening to his songs, but this was the first time they witnessed him singing.

A Florida judge went so far as to call Elvis a "savage" who was corrupting the youth of the day and Elvis was forbidden to shake his body at a local gig. In response, Elvis gyrated his hips as well as his finger.

In 1956 while performing on the Steve Allen Show, Elvis was asked to perform his hit tune "You Ain't Nothin but a Hound Dog", to an actual basset hound on stage. This was one of those times when Elvis was heard backstage shouting in rage at the humiliation he was expected to endure.

Chapter 2: Military Service

Elvis bought the mansion Graceland in 1957 for
$100,000, and soon after had a waterfall built
inside it. This was also the year that Elvis was
ordered to report to Kennedy Veterans Hospital
in Memphis, for his pre-induction physical.
Interestingly enough, the draft board in Memphis
held a press conference to announce that Elvis
had been classified 1A and would be drafted
later that year.

The whole world watched as both the Air Force and Navy tried their best to recruit Elvis into their respective branch of service. The Air Force tried hard to get him so they could use him with their recruiting efforts. The Navy, on the other hand, offered Elvis his very own specially trained "Elvis Company". Elvis, being the down home country boy he was, made the decision to be a regular "G.I. and serve with the rest of the boys.

Elvis received his official draft notice on December 20, 1957, and because he was in the middle of making the movie King Creole, requested and official deferment from the draft in order to complete the filming. Elvis was granted a deferment until March 20, 1958. His Mon & Dad, and close friends accompanied him when he reported to the draft board on March 24, 1958, at 6:30 in the morning along with twelve other recruits to be sworn in. Elvis and his new buddies were then bussed to Fort Chaffee, Arkansas to be processed. It was there that Elvis received his famous haircut, and coined the phrase to the media "Hair today, gone tomorrow".

Elvis received his first duty station, Fort Hood in Texas where he was assigned to General George Patton's old unit, "Hell on Wheels", the 2nd Armored Division. During the next few weeks after arriving, Colonel Tom Parker, Elvis's Business Manager received well over 5000 letters addressed to Elvis, now the most famous soldier on active duty.

In 1958 Elvis was sent back to Fort Hood for advanced tank training. In order to be near their son, Elvis's parents move to Texas, near the Army base.

On July 2, 1958, "King Creole" opens in theaters around the United States and is a big hit. The reviews of the film and of Elvis become the best he will ever have during his career for acting. It was said that Elvis was to become a serious respected actor, something he could only dream of. Of course, as time would tell, that was a dream Elvis would never see come true. It was soon after the release of King Creole that Gladys Presley; Elvis's mother became ill and passed away on August 14, 1958. Her funeral was held in Memphis, with Elvis in attendance. This was one of the lowest times in Elvis's life.

After the funeral Elvis returned to the base and was assigned to the Third Armored "Spearhead" Tank Division, owners of the famous motto "Victory or Death". They were located in Friedberg, Germany, and that's where Elvis headed first on a troop train from Texas, then onboard the U.S.S. Randal to Germany where he was assigned to the Ray Kaserne Barracks, with Company C, a scout platoon. While Elvis was stationed in Germany, he portrayed the life of the average Joe serviceman, however, because of his financial situation, he was allowed to live off base, not in the barracks. This also allowed him to send for his father and Grandmother to live with him in his house in Germany.

Elvis continued to perform his duties in the Army just like all the other troops, and then some it is said. He was always concerned that people would think that he was receiving special treatment in the Army, so on many occasions he did more than required. He never wanted to be treated like a movie and recording celebrity. Elvis was dedicated to the job and earned his medals for marksmanship while in Germany.

It was while stationed in Germany that Elvis met his future wife Priscilla Ann Beaulieu, then 14 years old at a party he held at his home. Priscilla was the stepdaughter of Captain Joseph Beaulieu stationed at the air base in Friedberg, Germany.

The year 1959 starts with a bang for Elvis with an interview by American Bandstands Dick Clark via telephone for ABC-TV on Elvis's 24th birthday. With his new manager Colonel Parker, Elvis's career stays active with guest shots, promos and additional hit song releases. He rubs elbows with many stars in Europe and some famous people too and even poses with March of Dimes poster child. Elvis was also interviewed by Stars and Stripes magazine while still in Germany. During the interview when asked about serving with the other regulars instead of performing for the troops, Elvis smiles as he gave his answer. "Well. I was in a funny position. Actually that's the only way it could be. People were expecting me to goof up in one-way or another. They thought I wouldn't take it and so forth, and I was determined to go to any limits to prove otherwise, not only to the people who were wondering, but to myself".

After his return from Germany, and while stationed at Fort Dix, New Jersey, Elvis received his honorable discharge from the Army after serving 18 months in Germany. He had earned a Sergeant's rank, E-5, and his muster out check was $109.54, quite a bit of money back then. Elvis, as well as his fans, were ready for him to be back home, producing new music and movies.

You can probably imagine that there aren't many people on the face of the earth that haven't heard of Elvis Presley at least as a singer, and maybe as an actor. But something most people don't fully understand was his dedication to Martial Arts. He was introduced to them while stationed in Germany while in the Army. When Elvis was discharged in 1960, he already had attained his first black belt in Karate.

You could say that Elvis had always been a "hands on" kind of guy, with a history before entering the military for using his fists on two recorded situations. Both had been in self-defense, and although there were charges against him they were dropped. During his early years before becoming "The King", Elvis sang in clubs all over the southern states, where he often had to defend himself.

As you look at his career both in movies as well as on stage performing, many of his poses especially during the 1970's were actually martial arts poses. In fact, when his gospel album released by the name "His Hand in Mine", it showed Elvis on the cover wearing his black belt pin on his lapel. As his movie career progressed, so did his martial arts in competitions as well as on the big screen. Just watch on of his films like G.I Blues, Blue Hawaii and Kid Galahad, where Elvis assisted to choreograph the fight scenes, and you can see the Karate moves.

While blocking a kick in the filming of G.I. Blues, Elvis had injured his hands with incorrect blocking, and his hands swelled up like balloons. As a matter of a fact, you can actually see his swollen hands in the back cover photo of the soundtrack for the movie. That crazy longhaired kid from Memphis could never stop showing off his Martial Arts skills, especially to his fans. He used to put on demonstrations breaking bricks with his bare hands before concerts.

Chapter 3: Commercial Success

An interesting fact related to Elvis happened because of his song Return to Sender in 1962. Thirty years later in 1992 a commemorative Elvis stamp was released in the United States. People rushed to purchase the stamps, and use them on letters with wrong addresses so they would receive the letter back market "return to sender".

In 1966 Elvis signs an extension with MGM for four more movies and in February stars in his 22nd movie "Spinout" along with doing the soundtrack. During this time, Elvis decided to update his band and recording equipment, and begins recording at Graceland with band members Red and Charlie. This is also the year that Elvis buys his Greyhound Bus and has it customized for performing on the road.

During 1966, Elvis stars in multiple films including "Double Trouble", "Paradise Hawaiian Style" "Easy Come, Easy Go" and more, none of which do well in theaters. His soundtracks never make it any higher than 15 on the charts.

Elvis has been dating Priscilla now for quite some time, and in December of 1966 he proposes with a fine diamond ring, just before Christmas. Also around this time, Elvis becomes seriously interested in horses and starts buying everything associated with them. A visit to Graceland today, will prove his love of horses, as they still run freely on the property after all these years.

Elvis finds a 163-acre ranch in Mississippi in February of 1967, and purchases it for himself, and his entire entourage of people and their families to live on. He purchases a horse for Priscilla, and many of his associates wives who along with Priscilla have become equestrians also. As the amount of people and horses have overgrown Graceland, the Circle G becomes their haven, where Elvis spends quite a bit of time. As his career takes a steady trend downward, the Circle G becomes his escape from the frustration because of the peak of his success.

1967 continues to be a good year for Elvis, with the release and Grammy Award for his gospel song "How Great Thou Art". Three more movies open for Elvis, Double Trouble, Easy Come, Easy Go and Clambake, none of which do very well.

This is also the year that Elvis and Priscilla get married, on May 1st in a very private ceremony in Las Vegas at the Aladdin Hotel with a small breakfast reception following the wedding. Following the wedding in Vegas, Elvis and Priscilla Presley honeymoon for a few days in Palm Springs, then return to Graceland. Later that month they slip into their wedding clothes and hold a second wedding reception at Graceland for all their family and friends who didn't get to attend the wedding. Later that month they would purchase their first home together, in Beverly Hills California, for $400,000, a great deal of money in the 1960's.

One day in 1968 Elvis was walking down a busy street in Los Angeles and realized not one person approached him in recognition. Elvis was in need of a giant comeback, and he and his manager Parker booked a performance in Burbank, California that started just that. This prompted a special on TV that re-launched his career. He also released four hits, "In the Ghetto", "If I can Dream", "Suspicious Minds", and "He Touched Me".

Elvis became close friends with many of the Memphis Mafia and actually gave Karate instructions to many of them. In fact, he eventually hired some of them as bodyguards. In a playful fight with actor Red West, previously a Memphis Mafia member, Elvis broke Red's arm. His love of the sport prompted him to finance the Tennessee Karate Institute, along with providing all funding for the 1974 U.S. Karate Teams World Tour. Although Elvis was never able to go on the Karate Tournament's worldwide because of his movies and singing career, he did keep in excellent shape. Having many serious accidents performing his own stunts in movies, Elvis seemed to avoid serious injury because of his Karate. Even after Elvis began to lose the battle of middle age and weight gain, he was still able to hold his own on the martial arts mat.

Elvis showed the world that not only could he rock your world on the sound stage, however, he could rock your world if you faced him on the fighting mat.

In January of 1970, a who new Elvis returns to Las Vegas at the International Hotel for a month of shows. It's the introduction of Elvis in his iconic one-piece jumpsuits and Karate moves during his performances. Also during February and March Elvis performs in Houston Texas at the Astrodome, where he is presented with multiple gold album awards. The performances draw crowds in excess of 200,000 fans and sets audience records. It is rumored at this time that Elvis might be looking at taking to the road on tour, something he hadn't done since the 1950's.

Justifying all rumors, Elvis takes his band on the road for a nine-city tour in September of 1970. The tour is a massive success for him, and MGM Studios records portions of the tour for an upcoming special: Elvis-That's the Way It Was".

During the rest of 1970, Elvis rides high on his newfound success, and starts purchasing high-end limited edition cars, starting with a Stutz Blackhawk, the new 1971 model. He and wife Priscilla also purchase a second home in California for $339,000, and expensive jewelry for Priscilla in Beverly Hills. However, the real highlight for Elvis is his famous visit to the White House and personally visiting President Richard Nixon. Even today, the photo's taken of Elvis and Nixon is requested from our National Archives in Washington.

1971 sees Elvis attending multiple award ceremonies, along with another gig in Las Vegas at the International Hotel. In March Elvis along with nine other awardees, receives recognition from the Jaycees, as one of the Top Ten Outstanding Young Men of the nation. This was one of the most touching moments in Elvis's life because he grew up dirt poor, scoffed and ridiculed with nothing but criticism for his work until now. It is quite possible that this moment was an inspiration for his hit song, "Follow that Dream".

Also this year, Elvis is honored on the cover of "Look Magazine" featuring an article on the release of his biography titled "Elvis: A Biography" which was released towards the end of the year.

The 1980's say the opening of Graceland to the public and his record sales reaching one billion worldwide. In 1986 at the first induction dinner of the Rock and Roll Hall of Fame, Elvis is inducted.

Chapter 4: Film Career

Let's look back at the history of Elvis Presley on the Big Silver Screen.

All in all, Elvis starred in 31 movies as an actor, along with two documentary films, Elvis That's the way it was, and Elvis On Tour.

His first movie was **Love Me Tender** in 1956 with Twentieth Century Fox, which premiered in November of that year. It was a western movie set in the days right after the Civil War. As movie history will show, this was the only film in which Elvis didn't have the No. 1 starring role, but was, in fact, second billing to Richard Egan. A fun fact about this film is that it was originally named "The Reno Brothers". However Elvis's song "Love Me Tender" which was to be used in the film sold over a million copies before the movie release. To maximize on this phenomenon, the producers decided to change the name to the song title. The character Elvis played was Clint Reno, whose character is killed in the movie. Although there was an attempt to splice in a different scene to keep Elvis alive because of his fame, it wasn't done, thus Elvis does die in the movie.

In 1957, Elvis starred in **Loving You** with Paramount Studios.

Of note, this was the first movie that Elvis starred in filmed in full color. You find the actor in Elvis more realistic in Loving You, mainly because this film actually depicted real-life experiences of Elvis's past. In this film, Elvis plays a singing truck driver who finds success in a country western band. With multiple love interests in the film, Elvis ends with outstanding success in the role. Again for this film, the name started out as Lonesome Cowboy, then changed to Running Wild, and finally released as Loving You. Loving you premiered in Memphis in July at the Strand Theater; however, Elvis didn't attend it there. He instead had a private midnight screening with his girlfriend Anita Wood and his parents.

A Special note for the year 1957, this was the year that Elvis Presley decided to dye his hair from his natural light brown, to the dark black we all remember him for. His inspiration for friend Tony Curtis, who also died his hair black was the decision maker. Only once in the rest of Elvis's life would he let his hair go back to natural light brown. That was while he was in the Army from 1958-1960.

His next film was Jailhouse Rock filmed in 1957 by Metro-Goldwyn-Mayer. In this movie, Elvis plays Vince Everett, sent to prison for Manslaughter, whose cellmate was a country western singer. Vince forms a bond with his cellmate and after release from prison, Elvis joins his band, and on to success, fame and fortune. During the filming of this movie, rumors stated that Elvis choreographed the film; however, actually he didn't. However, the film script called for Elvis to use Fred Astaire type moves, which they found just didn't work for Elvis's hips! The actual choreographer decided to watch Elvis preform "Hound Dog" and "All Shook Up", and after seeing how Elvis moved, he re-worked the moves to be more natural for Elvis.

During the filming of Jailhouse Rock, Elvis Pressley's singing career could have ended, during a freak accident. Elvis was sliding down a pole and lost a cap off a tooth, which he inhaled into a lung. A surgeon had to part Elvis Presley's famous vocal cords to remove the dental cap, which he did successfully. For days after surgery Elvis was raspy voiced. Unbelievably, the part he was cast as, Vice Everett in the film has an injury to his vocal cords and is hoarse also. It appears some things happen in strange manners.

During the filming of Jailhouse Rock, the cafeteria added to the menu one of Elvis's favorite meals, crispy bacon, mashed potatoes and brown gravy.

Also, there was a fire in co-star Jennifer Holden's dressing room. It was Elvis who ran in and came out carrying her to safety. And for those who have seen or heard of the classic movie Thunder Road, starring Robert Mitchum, here is some trivia. Mitchum visit Elvis during the filming of Jailhouse, and asked Elvis to star as his son in Thunder Road. Elvis never did do that part.

In 1958, Elvis starred in King Creole filmed by Paramount Studios. During this film, he starred alongside such famous actors and actresses as, Walther Matthau and Vic Morrow. This film became known as one of Elvis's best acting examples of his entire career, based on a Harold Robbins novel, "A Stone for Danny Fisher". It was during the filming of this movie, in New Orleans, that security and isolation started becoming a way of life for the now famous Elvis. Fans flooded New Orleans to just get a peek at the star, and the entire top floor of the Roosevelt Hotel was secured for the entire cast. Pinkerton guards were hired to secure the hotel, elevators and staircases, keeping fans out. It was during this filming that Elvis began eating all meals in his room. His worst experience was when he really wanted to eat at the world famous Antoine's Restaurant, but because there was no guarantee of crowd control, he had to cancel.

Elvis starred in GI Blues in 1960, with Paramount Studios.

Who would of guess that after two years in the Army Elvis would star in a movie about the Army set in Germany, entitled G.I. Blues. One month after being discharged from active duty, Elvis started filming in California. Actually some footage was filmed in Germany before Elvis left Germany while still stationed in Germany. Although Elvis didn't appear in the footage, actual filming of tanks and supply crews were. In G.I. Blues, Elvis played the part of Tulsa MacLean, an Army Sergeant stationed in Germany.

This was to be Elvis's first musical production. Film Director Norman Taurog directed this film, and proceeded to direct Elvis's next eight films. It is believed that Elvis's daughter Priscilla appeared as one of the children in the movie during the child puppet show.

As Elvis Presley grew in the world of the famous, so did his list of fans improve? While filming on set for G.I. Blues, Elvis was visited by Kings and Queens from all over the world. King Bumiphol and Queen Sirkik from Thailand, Princess Astrid of Norway, Princess Margaretha of Sweden and Princess Margretha of Denmark among them.

Elvis started mingling with other famous stars of the time, hitting the shows and lots of both Bobby Darin and Sammy Davis Jr., and even attended Dean Martin's birthday party.

It was also at this time that Elvis sent a request to the U.S. Army, asking if he could have his reserve status changed from active reserve to standby reserve. His request was granted.

It was around this time that Elvis's agent "The Colonel" Parker decided that Elvis needed to clean up his act. Elvis started appearing well-dressed and clean cut, no longer sporting long sideburns and gaudy "hip attire". The loss of sideburns pleased the press who produced some pretty awful comments about them over the years. If Elvis were alive today to see the likes of Kid Rock, Madonna and Dennis Rodman and their "attire", being celebrities, he would be astonished.

G.I. Blues management team made some subtle improvements to Elvis on screen, creating a whole new more mature older character. You can also see that Elvis no longer swayed and swung his hips as he sang.

In 1960 Elvis filmed Flaming Star with co-star Barbara Eden and produced Flaming Star by Twentieth Century Fox, his sixth movie to date. This was a movie slated for Marlon Brando about a young man with a white father and Indian mother. The original movie was named Black Star but was changed to make it more appealing to commercials. This movie was a basic "shoot em up" cowboy and Indian film set in the old west. With many more name changes as well as possible "leading man" choices, Elvis finally agreed to make the film. Elvis produced the theme song, "Black Star" for the movie, and then the name of the film was again changed to Flaming Star. Elvis was put to the task of re-inventing the song with the new name.

It was during filming of this film that Elvis's love of horses flourished. He started taking lessons to improve his riding skills, and was thrown many times, but never injured. He also was forced to be fitted with brown contact lenses for the movie to cover up his blue eyes. There was no such thing as a blue eyed Indian, and as this film was in color, Elvis wanted it real. This film was done on the set at Fox Studios as well as on the range of the Conejo Movie Ranch near Thousand Oaks, California.

As Elvis had recorded quite a few songs to be used in the movie, there was an advanced screening done in November before release of the movie. Based on polls at the screening, of these, "Britches", Winter Tears and Summer Kisses" we cut from the final released film. The film was quite the success for Elvis, reaching #12 on the movie charts. The Native American Council for the excellent way he portrayed the American Indian in the film also honored Elvis.

As a sign of the times back then, this Elvis movie was banned in South Africa because of the way it showed issues created by being in a bi-racial marriage.

Food for thought is the fact that Elvis did such an excellent performance in the lead of this film, which was meant for Marlon Brando, already a successful actor. Many say that had Elvis not been cast in so many musicals, and pursued a career as an actor, he would have become a Brando.

Again in 1960 just after completing Flaming Star, Elvis jumped into the production of "Wild in the Country", his seventh film. In this movie Elvis plays a young man that is sort of a rebel in his day named Glenn Tyler. This movie was supposed to be done as a drama, but because the star was Elvis, it was re-written for him as well as his songs created for the movie. All in all, Elvis recorded six songs for this movie, starting with the featured title song, Wild in the Country. During the final cut, two of the six were cut from the musical drama, Lonely Man and Forget Me Not. Remaining in the movie, Husky Dusky Day, I Slipped, I Stumbled, I Fell and In My Way. This movie premiered in Memphis on June 15th 1961, and as was often the case, Elvis didn't attend the premier of the film.

Of note in this film were two female co-stars, Tuesday Weld and Hope Lange, both well-known and accomplished actresses of the day.

A fact not known to many, even Elvis followers of today was the work Elvis did to make it possible for us to visit the USS Arizona Memorial in Hawaii. While Elvis was in production of Wild in the Country, Elvis learned from his manager who had read article in the newspaper of an attempt to raise funds to build the memorial above the massive underwater gravesite in Hawaii. Elvis and his manager "The Colonel" Tom Parker organized a benefit concert for the project, and managed to raise a whopping $62,000, which proved to be the largest donation to this hugely important project. The publicity of a successful benefit concert by Elvis, which hit all the news sources, spread the country and renewed interest in the project. The result is the incredible war memorial you can visit today. In all likelihood, without the donation by Elvis, this project and awesome memorial to those who died at Pearl Harbor, might not be there today.

Another thing of interest that occurred during the filming of Wild in the Country was the celebration of Elvis Presley's 26th birthday on the set. His crew and cast presented Elvis with a plaque to celebrate this day, which read, "Happy Birthday King Karate". You see, Elvis got an interest in martial arts while serving in the Army in Europe, and never really got it out of his system. In fact, Elvis earned the coveted 1st Degree Black Belt in 1960. Before Elvis died, he would go on to be awarded two 8th Degree Black Belts, in two different forms of martial arts.

Also in 1961 Elvis Presley filmed in Hawaii the hit musical production "Blue Hawaii", on location on the islands of Kauai and Oahu. This film and its songs became a hit throughout the world and was on the lips of many a person for years. It, in fact, became Elvis's biggest and most financially successful film ever. Just the soundtrack along brought tremendous success to the Elvis financial coffer, with the album on top of the charts for almost eighty weeks, and number one for over twenty weeks.

Again this film started with a different title, "Hawaiian Beach Boy", but was later changed to Blue Hawaii. For anyone who has watched this movie, or will be watching it, the wedding scene will forever be in your memory as just beautiful. It was filmed on location at the Coco Palms Resort on Kauai. For anyone wanting to re-create this wedding on site, sorry, the resort closed its doors after devastation in the 1992 hurricane Iniki. An interesting fact about the spot that this resort was built on, is who lived there previously. On this site Queen Deborah Kapule, the last of her kind, lived in her ancestral home.

Two of Elvis Presley's co-stars are noteworthy; Roland Winters had portrayed Charlie Chan in many movies, and Angela Lansbury star in many movies, quite notably, Murder She Wrote.

An interesting fact for the younger generations is to remember that Hawaii at the time of this filming had only been a state for two years. That's right, they officially became the State of Hawaii in 1959. That being said, the new State of Hawaii was quite eager to get some free exposure, and boy did they ever with the film Blue Hawaii. Everyone that watches this film, even today, and has never been to the Hawaiian Islands starts to plan a trip. The movie gave future vacationers a view of Waikiki Beach, the Coco Palms Resort, and Ala Moana Park as well as some of the most beautiful beaches in the world, as well as beautiful waters and waves. The movie even gave the world a glimpse of what the inside of Honolulu Jail looks like, somewhere they didn't want to visit on their vacation.

During the filming of Blue Hawaii, again we saw the constant battering of Elvis and his crew by fans, constantly creating issues and again putting the star in hiding. It's interesting and in some cases disappointing to see that still today, these same problems haunt the stars, causing them to become reclusive, and leading to some pretty unhealthy habits. But back to Elvis.

Every day starting with the day Elvis arrived at the airport there were security issues. Mobs broke down barricades to get to him, and every day surrounded his hotel. The psychology of fame began to get to Elvis then as he used to watch vacationers outside his hotel on the beach, enjoying themselves. Elvis on the other hand, couldn't leave his hotel room to explore the island, only leaving to go to the next scene being shot.

It was the success at the box office for Blue Hawaii that would keep him from becoming a serious actor, something Elvis really desired. His manager Colonel Parker persuaded Elvis that the only success he could see was singing in musicals and keeping the focus on his singing abilities and looks, not his acting. It's a pity that the world never actually had much of a chance to see what could have become of Elvis, had he turned the corner into mainly acting, while keeping his songs to just the music charts. As said many times, Elvis could possibly have become at least as great an actor as Marlon Brando, or greater.

The release in May of 1962 of Elvis's 9th musical production "Follow that Dream", was quite successful, but not quite as much as his previous, Blue Hawaii. It was filmed on location in different locations in the state of Florida. Elvis's arrival in Florida from Memphis was quite a parade, with Elvis in his chartered bus, followed by his personal limousine that towed his brand new ski boat behind it. Elvis stayed at the Port Paradise Hotel in Crystal River, Florida while filming this musical, the Crystal River being the reason for the ski boat. Watching this film you can't help but wonder if anyone sees the similarity in the part Elvis plays, with Lil Abner and his back woods family. That's exactly what the whole story line is about, the Kwimper Family, backwoods mix of orphans and squatters living on the river.

Of interest with the production of Follow that Dream, is that it is one of the very few films Elvis starred in, that was filmed entirely on location there in Florida. Although that may seem like a great place to film a movie, you must realize that the temperatures ranged from 90's to into the 100's. In fact, there was one week while filming that every day reached over 100 F. In one week, Elvis changed his shirt for the filming over twenty times. Wardrobe department earned their pay that day for sure.

Another issue that came upon the production was the fact that some scenes called for gambling machines in them. At the time of production gambling was outlawed and illegal in the State of Florida.

Funny how "star power" can accomplish things because all of a sudden, one of the local political gentlemen and some gambler associate just showed up with some one-arm bandits for the set. Nothing ever came of the illegal machines; after all, the show must go on.

In 1962 in collaboration with United Artist Studios, Elvis produced his 10th feature musical / film, Kid Galahad, which had been filmed partially at the end of1961. This film was, in fact, a remake of an original production way back in the 1930's that featured Humphrey Bogart and was the story of a boxer. The production did make money that year, reaching #9 in top grossing films and ended up ranking 37 for the whole year.

There were some particularly well known actors in this film too, from tough guy Charles Bronson to Ed Asner who achieved success as an actor later on the Mary Tyler Moore Show on TV.

Elvis was actually a perfect choice for this film manly because of how physically fit he kept himself with Karate. However, Elvis was no professional boxer, and he worked hard to prepare himself for this role. In accepting his role in this film, Elvis decided to live the life of a professional boxer, and did the road work, sparred with real boxers, and worked out on the punching bag. He lost twelve pounds and gained some muscle by the time of filming.

Elvis's eleventh film was titled "Girls, Girls, Girls" and, although filmed in beautiful Hawaii, was not bone of his favorite productions. Produced by Paramount Productions, it was expected to work out as well as Blue Hawaii, but eventually came up quite short of that. Producer Hal Wallis was extremely happy to have Elvis as an entertainer in the film instead of featuring him as a serious actor.

From the get go, Elvis wasn't happy with where his acting career was going. This film had started off with titles like Gumbo Ya-Ya, Jambalaya, Welcome Aboard and A Girl In Every Port, but settled on Girls, Girls, Girls. These titles sort of describe the theme of the production, which surrounded the main character Elvis, as a boat captain who sang in a club at night. The title song, Girls, Girls, Girls, had actually been written for another up and coming singing group, The Coasters. Elvis became increasingly upset with ideas like having him sing to a shrimp! However, there is one truly great thing that came from this movie, and that's his hit song "Return To Sender". Actually not written to be performed in this movie, when Parker heard it he decided it was a perfect song for Elvis to perform. As history would show, Elvis's manager was correct. Like we stated earlier, it was this hit song that prompted hundreds of fans to send letters to the wrong address, just to get the "return to sender" stamped on the letter or postcard.

For the filming of this movie in Hawaii, again as always Elvis was mobbed at the airport as well as his hotel, the Hawaiian Village Hotel. There were over 8,000 fans waiting at the hotel when Elvis arrived in style, in a helicopter. His walk through "the gauntlet" of fans some 100 yards to the entrance of the hotel was a zoo. As he finally scrambled through the front doors, he had lost his favorite yachting hat, a jeweled tie clasp and most importantly his favorite diamond ring.

The diamond ring was left at the front desk for Elvis by a young female fan the next day.

After filming in Hawaii was completed, Elvis and the crew returned to Hollywood to finish the production. Here, Elvis actually started to enjoy himself, fan free. He was able to play football with friends, including Pat Boone, Ricky Nelson and others on weekends in a local park. Elvis was also getting truly serious about staying in shape, as well as working out with Karate. He argued and eventually lost to producer Hal Wallis, over the 40+ boards Elvis would break with his hands each day. The fear was he would break his wrist or hand and be out of the film.

It Happened at the World's Fair was Elvis's 12th movie in collaboration with MGM Studios and was filmed on set in Seattle, Washington in 1963 during the actual World's Fair. Actually, back then it wasn't called that, rather it was titled the Seattle Century 21 Exposition. To get an idea of what was spend on the actor's wardrobe for his productions, this film spent over $9000 on Elvis's wardrobe. It consisted of some 30 shirts, 50+ ties, coats and jackets and 15 pair of slacks. This was a lot of money back in the 1960's you have to remember, and on our scale today would have been at least triple that or more.

As far as security for this filming, it was nothing short of that for a president. Elvis now always traveled with his own private security team, but, in addition, hundreds of area law enforcement and Pinkerton Agents in street clothes were added to protect Elvis in crowds.

An interesting tidbit about Elvis and his pals staying at the hotel was a favorite joke they played. Many times they would be hotel bound because of fans so they would get bored quite often. One of the things they enjoyed doing in a new hotel was to call for room service, then remove all furniture in the room. When the server arrived with the food cart, he or she was astounded to find all the guys sitting on the floor. Leaving to get the hotel manager, upon returning they would find everything back in place.

Another interesting thing from this movie was the introduction of now famous actor Kurt Russell, who played a ten-year-old boy who kicks Elvis in the shin in the movie. Many years later that same little boy Kurt Russell would play the part of Elvis Presley in a TV Movie about the star.

It was during the time that this movie was released that the public realized there had been a substantial change in Elvis Presley. No longer the Rock Star that he started out being, he had been groomed and developed into a leading man for film. His wardrobe had changed dramatically, with suits and ties, no sideburns, and dress slacks. This was all the work of a man named Sy Devore, a well known Hollywood Tailor to the stars who had been given the task of re-creating the Elvis we all knew and loved. His task at hand, to morph Elvis from that rough around the edges, swinging hipped rebel, into a "smart, well-dressed young businessman".

Elvis's next production was Fun in Acapulco in 1963, staring Elvis as an ex-circus performer getting away from the circus after an accident. Arriving in Mexico he takes a position as a lifeguard, a singing lifeguard to be exact, singing to guests in the evenings. As part of the screen write, Elvis's character is involved romantically with two beautiful ladies, one the hotel social director and the other a female bullfighter. He decides to stick to one and choses the manager, who, by the way, was played by Ursula Andress, who at the time was considered to be one of the most beautiful young ladies around.

It's interesting to note that during the filming of this movie, Elvis demanded that he perform his own stunts many that were considered dangerous. Some were performed on a trapeze 20 feet above the floor without a net, which scared the producers to no end. They decided to do the filming of those at the very end, just in case of an accident, so they could re-take with a double. One of the stunts that Elvis decided not to perform was the death-defying leap off the cliffs at La Quebrada, which is a 136-foot cliff dive.

Kissing Cousins released in 1964 with MGM was interesting in the fact that it was Elvis's first time playing a dual role. In this movie, Elvis played twins, one with black hair, one with blonde. As history would show, this movie was reported to be Elvis's worst movies, and was rumored to have been a rushed filming, low budget mess. This film was filmed in only two weeks with a budget under $1 million dollars, you can compare this to the highly successful Blue Hawaii with its budget of over $4 million.

During the filming of Kissing Cousins, which was partially filmed in Big Bear, California, Elvis proved his weight as a driver. Driving his own motorhome down the mountain it lost brakes, and only by his skills was he able to use the gears to slow down and not go off a cliff.

One of Elvis Presley's most notable movies and a song he performed the rest of his life, and still famous today, was Viva Las Vegas. This musical is considered by most to be his best ever. The movie was to become his highest grossing film ever starred in by Elvis. The song Viva Las Vegas, performed by Elvis is still being used today in the hit TV show "Vegas". Co-staring in this film was Ann –Margaret who has turned men's heads her whole life. The film was done on location in Las Vegas, at locations like the Sahara Hotel, Lake Meade, skeet shooting at the Tropicana Hotel, the pool of the Flamingo and others.

Even though Elvis was seeing his soon to be wife Priscilla who remained back in Memphis, Elvis had a quite public affair with Ann Margaret during filming. Although at first Elvis didn't want to co-star with her, her attraction just overcame him, although it is believed he broke it off because of his love for Priscilla. Elvis and Ann remained close friends for the remainder of his life.

From 1964 to 1969 Elvis played starring roles in sixteen more musicals, some notable, some not so much. Roustabout, Frankie and Johnny, Spinout, The Trouble With Girls were some of the more note worthy of them. Elvis would find none of the success he had found previously in his big hits.

Elvis played his last on screen role in the movie Change of Habit in 1969 produced by Universal Studios. As luck would have it, something Elvis always wanted to do, star in a dramatic role, his last film was just that. Not much singing in this production, only three songs actually. Elvis plays the part of a Doctor in the ghetto, and this is the first and only film where Elvis is dressed like a professional man, suite and tie.

Chapter 5: The Comeback

When Elvis Presley rolled into the town of Las Vegas to make it his home for the remainder of his years as an entertainer, it was spectacular. Loudspeakers bellowed the words on the streets, "Elvis has arrived in town, and he's here to stay. Las Vegas will never be the same". It was now almost a decade after his filming career had ended, and Elvis was planning to revive himself in Vegas. Nothing could have been further from the truth. He did make a difference, and Las Vegas did thrive because he was there, but Las Vegas was what brought Elvis down, in many opinions.

Elvis opened his Vegas career at the new International Hotel, which later became the Hilton. His show was such a success that later that night he ordered to be brought to his room, 30 diamond studded Rolex watches, which he passed out to his entourage. He then bought 14 Cadillac's, and presented them to his 14 closest friends. Elvis lived high, in more ways than one. Elvis started rolling in the money, paid $100,000 a week, big money back then.

As Elvis began helping the town of Las Vegas grow, Las Vegas helped Elvis's belly to grow in return. Those that remember seeing Elvis back then in Vegas, in person or on TV, remember his white jumpsuits. It seemed that between only a few performances, wardrobe would be required to expand his suits. We can remember the jumpsuits not being plain, rather covered with gemstones, which added at times 20-30 lbs. to his outfit.

As Elvis became caught up in the lifestyle of the town, as well as having to deal with the pain and frustration of his medical issues, the drugs started to take their toll. On stage, Elvis would start slurring his words, forget his own lyrics and ramble on. As has been the case over and over in time with stars of the screen and music charts, medications were abundant, and often over prescribed. Elvis had five physicians prescribing medications for him, and none of them were aware of each other.

Elvis had not waited until arriving in Las Vegas at this late in the game to get into drugs. The fame and fortune of being a star, on the road, gave him access to drugs for many years, although by the early 1970's he was taking amphetamines, barbiturates and other painkillers.

It's so sad to see what a young and talented man from a bad part of town so to speak, could bring himself to such a high level of success and fame, only to fall because of addiction to drugs. Sad also that we see this over and over almost every time we turn on TV it seems.

All in all, Elvis's last years performing in Las Vegas were some of his best and worse. After performing his 837th show in Las Vegas, Elvis left for his home at Graceland, getting his newly planned U.S. Concert Tour ready for that following summer. He would never perform in Las Vegas again, or anywhere else for that matter.

On August 16th, 1977, Elvis was discovered by his staff at the Graceland mansion, collapsed on the floor of his bathroom. He was transported to the Baptist memorial Hospital where several attempts were made to revive him, but he was pronounced dead at 3:30 PM. There were many contributing factors to the cause of death for Elvis, as well as multiple reports based on different factors. The autopsy itself determined that Elvis did, in fact, have narcotics in his bloodstream, including painkillers, tranquilizers, as well as sleeping medication comprised of Codeine and other barbiturates.

The reason for many of these drugs being taken by Elvis in large quantities, have been argued by many professionals, as has the real cause of death. Whether it was as most believe, an addiction for sleeplessness, or pain medication for a medical condition of the bowels, the fact is that Elvis was injecting large quantities of drugs. We have seen this over and over in the world of the rich and famous, most recently in the life and death of Michel Jackson.

Officially, the coroner's office reported that Elvis died from a "cardiac arrhythmia", which was later changed to reflect an end result of a cocktail of ten prescribed drugs that caused the cardiac problem. The medical term "cardiac arrhythmia" means only that the heart has stopped, and not what caused it to start. It is believed that the family of Elvis Presley, as well as the physicians performing the autopsy, tried to portray that his heart just stopped.

The plain fact is that an abuse of drugs was the cause of Elvis Presley's death, plain and simple. A compounding factor that could have been associated with his overdose was the fact that on the 15th of August, his dentist gave him codeine. Some that this resulted in Elvis going into anaphylactic shock from the drug, which had happened once before, believed it.

In later years longtime friend and physician Dr. George Nichopoulos wrote a book about Elvis's life and death, and revealed something not openly known to friends or fans. For most of his life Elvis suffered from a chronic intestinal disease that not only caused him issues on stage but off stage, as well. Elvis was advised by his medical advisors later in life to have a surgical procedure to relieve this situation; however, Elvis refused. The reasons, it appears, for the refusal, was Elvis was more concerned with what his public would think, instead of how it would change and improve his quality of life.

There is also a major consensus that in his later years, when Elvis appeared and was, in fact, mush heavier than he had ever been, that his medical condition probably had a lot to do with the weight gains also.

In the end, there is a remarkably good possibility that this medical condition contributed to the cause of Elvis's death at such an early age.

Chapter 6: Death and Legacy

Elvis's legacy lives on today, over thirty-five years after his death where it is no wonder that Elvis, the original "American Idol", can still be found in show business. On the radio, television, and his songs being used for hit TV series shows such as "Vegas" with the Elvis hit song "A Little Less Conversation". It's special to see that a country boy from a family, who experienced such hard times, could elevate himself to become one of the most sacred idols of our time.

Yes, Elvis Presley had his ups and downs as do most of us in life, but Elvis always had principals he lived by. Even during those not so bright days when he fell to a life of drugs, most often prescription from his doctors, Elvis was trying to guide others. He used his name and influence to bring the bad about drug use to the public, and even worked with the President of the United States on a program about addiction.

His later years were filled with the tabloids talking about his drugs and weight, violence and guns. Anyone that can remember seeing Elvis on television, Vegas or National Inquirer at the local market, remember Elvis being very heavy in a white jumpsuit. Even in those times, Elvis drew sold out crowds at his shows, with ladies in the audience screaming his name, and praying they get one of his white silk towels he threw down to spectators.

After his death, his movies and songs survived the bad press, stories around his death and life, and even today you can listen to his music on the Elvis satellite channels. It doesn't matter what the tabloids or media said about the fans that still idolized him, or those that even today are making money off Elvis memorabilia.

Recording giant RCA continued over the years to release commemorative albums of Elvis's songs, like the "Elvis: 30 #1 Hits album that roared to the #1 slot on the charts and sold over 500,000 copies, the first week, and that was twenty five years after his death. These thirty top songs from his life spanned time from early in his career, 1956 with "Heartbreak Hotel" all the way to 1977 with "Way Down". So this album totally demolishes the statements of the industry that claim Elvis's career fizzled towards the end of his life. Heck, he was producing hit songs the year before his death.

In order to create the Elvis: 30 #1 Hits album, it was necessary to pull the original tapes, from the archives at RCA's storage facility in Pennsylvania. Now you have to understand that these originals were recorded on reel-to-reel tape systems on recording tape. This was used long before the DVD, cassette or other modern recording devices used today.

Many of these tapes in the storage unit hadn't been played in over 40 years and were in pretty bad shape. Most were actually repaired and transferred to a digital format, where they were repaired for sound quality. In fact, some of the tapes were so oxidized that they were put into an oven to seal the oxidation on the surface. Once they were digitized, advances in todays technology allowed the songs to be enhanced for sound, because the originals, many recorded in mono had bad sound qualities. Another factor that influenced the songs that came out of the sound study during recording sessions was the fact that Elvis was in charge. All decisions were made in the studio, not before, and there was no piecing together takes, rather what recorded was what you got.

In 1977 at the time of Elvis's death, the King had sold over 250 million records. Like so many other stars, when they are gone, their stuff becomes not only valuable but also rare. Such was life after Elvis, as all of his records in stores sold out, as did any other memorabilia. Worldwide record pressing factories for RCA Records operated around the clock in most cases trying to keep up with orders for "The Kings" records, to the point that Elvis songs started hitting the charts again. In some cases companies producing records for multiple artists dropped production on others and focused on Elvis records.

Over the years, RCA Records has continued to produce Elvis record albums at a rate of maybe 2-3 per year, and selling them. During the process of going through the storage vaults of Elvis's original recordings, RCA actually found many un-released songs, and started to release albums labeled "previously un-released". A major find for RCA was when they discovered a stash of tapes and records hidden at Graceland, which included interviews and stage recordings. On the anniversary of Elvis's 50th Birthday, RCA released a 6- Album record set. The year was 1983.

When Bertlesmann Music Group purchased RCA shortly after that, they continued the Elvis Legacy releasing Elvis records and over years multiple silver and gold records were awarded to Elvis the American Idol.

During the 1990's multiple albums were released, named the "Masters Series" with collections from the 50's, 60's and 70's all on CD's.

The legacy that is Elvis comes not only from his music, but also from the connection he seemed to make on his fan base. He was a rebel of his times, and even after all these years after his death, when you see one of his movies show up on your cable TV, there's just something about Elvis. It's his moves, his deep voice, jet black long slicked hair. Whatever it is, slap a song of his on your iPod or a photo of him on your iPad, and pretty much anyone will tell you who it is. Another reason Elvis lives today is because of his fan base, fan clubs and memories Elvis created.

The thought of Hawaii or Las Vegas brings thoughts of Elvis from his movies and shows, even today.

In 2002, Elvis hit the Top Ten Charts again, after the re-mix of his hit song "A Little Less Conversation" was used by Nike in a commercial for the "World Cup".

The King Lives On…